Following Fred Astaire

Winner of the 1998 Washington Prize

THE WORD WORKS
Washington, D.C.

NATHALIE F. ANDERSON

Nathalie F. Anderson
IOTA
Dec. 10, 2000.

First Edition
First Printing
Following Fred Astaire

Printed in the U.S.A.
Book design, typography by Janice Olson
Cover art: Detail of "Tea Party with Hermit Crabs," painting by Perky Edgerton

Library of Congress Number: 98-61425
International Standard Book Number: 0-915380-41-2

Acknowledgements

"Red Sea" originally appeared in *The Denver Quarterly*; "Lost Sisters," "Gazelles," and "Oralee Dantzler" in *Prairie Schooner*; "Aulophobia," "Erythrophobia," and "Nephophobia" in *The Paris Review*; "Koniophobia" and "Thalassophobia" in *Spazio Humano*; "Gymnophobia" and "Pogonophobia" in */~xconnect*; "Belenophobia, Enetophobia" in the *APR Philly Edition*; and "Afterlife," "Desire," "Loose Woman," and "Stick Shift" in *Southern Poetry Review.*

I am grateful to Yaddo, to Swarthmore College, and to the Pew Fellowships in the Arts for support in completing this manuscript; and to Karren Alenier, Abbe Blum, Betsy Bolton, Marcus Cafagña, Eileen Cahill, Chin Woon-Ping, Lisa Coffman, Gigi and Buzz Crompton, Peter Fallon, Bob FitzSimons, Daisy Fried, Dillon Johnston, Janice Olson, Lee and Edith Potter, Elena Retfalvi, Peter Schmidt, Kristina Straub, Hilary Tham, and Carrie Yamaoka for comfort and advice.

Contents

III

≈

IV

≈

For Kristina Straub

I

The Dream of Return

You have a friend in a distant country
and night after night she calls. Her longing
draws the nails from your door frame, the pintle
from the hinge, the key from the pocket where
you hid it, until here you are, air-borne.

When you arrive, the house is empty, bare
as always, dark as the hour of your birth.
How can you read the faceless woman
opening sheets for your white bed, as she
gestures you into the starless garden,

waste as only winter can make it? Here
you wait for a while, for a long while, as
longing draws the rings from your hands, shakes
the silver from your teeth, drags from your face
its hard-won lines. And here she is, your friend,

warm as your first lost blanket, the wool shrunk thick,
its dense length wound round and round, its arms so tight
it's as if you're in bed, sleeping, dreaming again
the dream of return. She's missed you so, she
longs to hold you—but here she is: your friend,

tapping your shoulder, eager for a turn,
surprised to see you so long before spring.
She takes your hand, as always, drawing you
in from the hedge thick with Christmas roses,
with winter jasmine, the sky with its own

white blooms. Who was it who held you? The house
overflowing, as always, with music,
laughter, friends—no strangers here. No one is
longing for you. No one but you is longing.
Night folds itself away. Where do you belong?

Reunion

Face it: nothing remains of yourself at seven,
that light hair unspooling in snips and threads,
that spot on your nail pushed out beyond reach.
Lungs have breathed themselves away, bowels unravelled.

Even those dreams of fire
that lit your sleep night after night
burned themselves out like tungsten.
No flint and steel, the filaments click.

And Edmund your cousin, whose walk you watched so long,
blurs in the thorn trees, a circuit nearly fused
while himself, at ease in a new body,
steps over the lawn in his old walk,
as much a stranger to himself as you.

Red Sea

She'd seen them before—
just boys from school.
No need to cross the street.

No need to guard her eyes—
though what darts aimless as a fish
will strike as blindly.

No snickering blade,
no smirk of broken glass.
Still, the cuts gape
hungry as sea anemone,
sharp as brine.

Remembering that day at the water fountain
he showed what he held in his hand—
a fish so bright
she lost the barb in its shining—

not bothering to watch her
listing among the lockers
lost in a red sea

thinking what she'd do
if he took it out again.

Eight Fears:

1. Aulophobia

Fear of Flutes

Right or wrong. Three silver birches
bar the window. So nearly straight.
Wind thin as a shiv. Desperate
teeth behind their silver bar.

Grasp and twist. Silver splits, shreds, flays.
Diminuendo. Lips blister,
stops spew hoarse waxy curds. Spiked through,
the rag's scummy. Trill. Tremolo.

Keen, you were keen. Tense. Again tense.
Keep it shrill. Knife at the teeth, wind
like a shiv. Upright, unfallen.
Silver birch. Silver blade. Spike. Bleb.

2. Belenophobia, Enetophobia

Fear of Needles, Fear of Pins

Il faut distinguer, mamselle. How prick
the accent: *grave? egue?* I gave my love
a paper of pins. How it starts, it's said.
Fold your paper. Prick it through: love's name.

Faux pas. I gave my love needles, pins.
Il faut distinguer. Head, eyes. Poisoned blood,
chipped bone. Granna stitched her thumb, red seaming
white folds. Fo fum. Teasing the splinter,

throbbing it out—ever do that? to
yourself? Picking clean the tailor's floor, found
differences: thistled fingers, pocked knees.
Rutting thumb. Stung nail. *Faut distinguer,* love.

3. Nephophobia

Fear of Clouds

Dead calm. They're on you before you feel them.
Flecked with them. Reek of the invisible
rasp, the livid trail. The sky's glaucous, blotched
with gleet. Creeping. Creeping.

Maggots. Slugs. Leeches. Pasty wraiths bloated,
leaden. And shifty—torpid turns turbid,
roils and spits, banks off into blear. Grizzled.
They're on you. Scuts, scuts spuming.

As the driven snow? as fleece? as feathers?
Sluts. Sluttish. On you before you feel them.
The brackish snuffle. Invisible rasp.
Slinking. Dissolute. Smut. Smut.

4. Gymnophobia

Fear of Nudity

Above us the Disco-Bats flicked their privates:
open, shut. Nothing we hadn't seen before.
Sequined, celestial: sissy-folk slip out, in.
Bird-women. Fly-boys. Starkers, snootfull of smooch.

Hoodwinked? Ha! Nothing we hadn't tried. False face,
nudish: each pricked veil, each spangled spread. Diddling
disguises—nothing we hadn't worn: romance,
lubricity. Cupid's eye-patch, coruscant.

Fly-by-nights. Short-falls. Bats swallow
their pleasures. Lippy muzzles, scintillant,
leap to the eye. Under the suck-guttle,
under the glut: feel it—the crawling skin.

5. Erythrophobia

Fear of Blushing

Oh ho she said. What's this I see. Red flag?
Blood and thunder? Bleeding heart? Smirk. Didder.
Rankles, does it? Galls? Don't slop over. Don't
gush. Quench it. Snuff it. Go dead-pan. Blue ruin.

Not how it looks. No blood-bath. No heart-throb.
A hairline fracture. A brain wave. Seepage.
Tremor. Melting point. Hot wind. Not heart-struck.
Not red-handed. Talk. Talk. Blue in the face?

Mayday. Mayday. Thin-skinned are you? Smirk. Smirch.
Squirm. Look at you. Gaudy. Deep-dye. Port wine.
Blot it up. Quench it. Snuff it out. Oh ho.
Shimmer, swelter, scorcher. Auto da fé.

6. Thalassophobia

Fear of the Sea

Glassy-eyed. Goblet, decanter: crystal's
sleek. Slips the grasp. Ching. Chink. Pinguidity.
Tap flumes; sink riffles with shoals. Blown glass, cut
glass: tip, tumble. Clitter. Splinter. Wrists slit.

Dishwater palms, lipped by slivers. Puckered,
stunned. Slim necks snap; sheer wells shiver. Swash. Swash.
Lucid? Luster. Beached brilliants glint, blink blind.
Spindrift, whitecaps: blown breakage. Smithereens.

Squalor. Ground glass, shattered, chatters under
foot. Backwash slithery, a satin scud.
Wrists slip back in the crush. Spritz. Crackle. Cut
glass, blown glass: glassy-eyed. The lassitude.

7. Koniophobia

Fear of Dust

Pick-face. Chapped, itching towards smoothness; blisters
crusted; scabs shucking bark; burnt white on red,
mica-brittle, mica-sheer; foxed corners
of a damp mouth: skin crumbs under her nail.

Skint. Brows fretted, stubble plucked thin, lashes
fished for. Scalp scratched clear of scurf; nose chafed, buffed,
fingered, thumbed, molted. Rusty blood chipped, hairs
scraped out in loving. Stale sleep scaled away.

What powders her face in the glass. What clouds
her pillow, breathless. What thickens, listless,
at the foot of the bed. What stares her down.
Defaced. Disfigured. Her mouth. Her eyes.

8. Pogonophobia

Fear of Beards

Shell delicate, the green chin's cracked: broken
waxwing, broken wryneck. The down ups, bristling,
kinking into curls. A fly-specked plaster,
a cambric snicked with stitches: this grizzling

frets against the grain. Scrit, scrit: the lie bare-faced,
the whiskered fibbery—lily-white boys, cheek
by jowl among the stubble. Peach-fuzz to
blue-beard, she's caught in their swart penumbra.

Like the gossamer thread sprung from her arm
a full three inches when she was eight, it
opened her eyes. Out of the glass each barb
of it speaks: Trust me. I hide what you are.

Walk Like a Man

for whoever it was—
Monroe Black? Taylor Garnett? Dick Manning?—
who tried to teach me, back in maybe 1963,
how to walk like the guys do.

"Sit
into it,"

he said, burlesquing squat and bounce
so I could see the torso pistoning,
the spine plunge, straight from head to hip,
like a rod in an engine, butt tucked,
legs bent to take the strain. "Sit

into it," shoving my shoulders down
so I could feel the brunt, feel the knees splay
at each step: instant cowboy, thighs rounding
an invisible horse. "Sit," the rise and fall
gradually levelling, the body riding

the legs' bobbery: swagger, saunter, stride.
All this for a walk-on at some girl's party,
and not what was wanted, after all: cute fluff
wambling in coat and tie. Still, for a week
I had it right. Not easy, keeping straight—

my body flung side to side, my hips
pitching it like a train on tight curves.
"With a swing like that," he said, "I'd never
leave home." And then, "Take a swig, grow
hair on your chest." Leaving home, growing hair,

fighting the sway—it was like dancing
with Holden Caulfield. Remember Holden? All that shit?
"No can, no legs, no feet—nothing beneath my hand"?
I used to practice dancing with him, full-length
in the bathroom mirror, clothes in a heap

by the filling tub, steam effacing feet, legs, can—
the perfect partner. Ass tucked under, weight
passed from leg to imperceptible leg,
the small of my back rounding to his
absent hand, he'd guide me all around the floor,

such as it was. Some guys appreciate it,
having a rod to hold—stiff as steel, brittle
as glass, the rigid back disclaiming the embrace,
refusing to cling. Not easy, keeping still
without the twitch that comes so naturally.

"Sit into it." You teach the body, and
then it teaches you, bucking like a bad horse
on some hacienda. Holden and them—
Monroe, Curtis, Taylor—almost never danced
for all that talk, spent all their time

sniggering in the dark. It's what boys do.
I never thought of walking over, sitting
in, sharing what passed from hand to hand
to hand. After all this time, it's hard to know
what difference it might make, what they might do.

Juke Box Memories

Just another couple making juke box memories
And walking into trouble hand in hand.
—Terry Allen

He used to play ball. Now he works the rodeo.
He has one question: what do you do for fun?

He asks every woman at the bar. I don't have the answers.
I read. I go to the movies. He keeps his eyes shut
when he dances.

I'm a real lady, he tells my friends at the table. It's not
an insult.
There's no doubleness in him, not like Cathy

her mouth closed on his tongue on the dance floor.
She reads too, but she won't say so.

He wants to work construction, he's that steady.
His hand's hot on my hip. He never moves it,

never insinuates himself. Take it
or leave it. Cathy does both. I believe

he's never seen me. He doesn't know my name.
He calls me honey. "Honey," he says

"Just because it's dark
don't mean I'm not looking."

Stick Shift

Sister Mary Odessa, Sister Sarah Choctaw
raising rival spirit hands at either end of
what was it? Kershaw or Cheraw—some main drag
where the low country shrugs into Piedmont,
where a girl might shift for herself, grinding her gears
from pillar to post, from post to pillar, bolt upright
against the pew back of her uncle's Oldsmobile.

Rounding the posts, snaking in and out of driveways,
she's notching the blacktop with her jarring stops, her
jack-rabbit starts, cheating the law and mother,
travelling without a license, gripping the wheel
as it writhes in her hands, sharp scales marking a palm
already scored by cotton bracts, tobacco twine—
a month, not a life, in the country. "Hold out your hand":

fool girl at the gates where nobody wants her,
pillar to post and post to pillar, queasy
on the roundabouts, dead at the wheel, overshooting
the home stretch. "Hold out your hand": the switch whistling,
the green bark fraying. One yard braced by white pickets,
flying prayer-wheels like pennons; the other oozing
foam flower, vine trumpet, blazing star. "Hold out your hand":

where witch water sluices the gully of the head,
the gully of the heart, pools in the well of the palm.
The past uncoils. The inexorable lies basking
sinuous and alien, where she'll have to back away
or run it down. Outside, tobacco's bolting
into bitterness, cotton's fraying, mother's
on her way. Say goodbye, Gretel. Hold out your hand.

Sister Mary Odessa, Sister Sarah Choctaw
I raise my red right hand to yours.
The road's rutted, witch water rising,
the blacksnakes swim with their heads above the ooze.
Whatever she told me won't hold water.
I'm travelling now, my eyes so full of sky
I take the road by braille.

The Dream of the Rose

You have a friend who knows what's best, and she
won't let you forget it. From interview
to interview she drags you round, famished
for the job she knows you need, you in your
pink A-line, boxy boiled-wool jacket, heels

that might be sensible for someone else,
cloaked in the good impression she knows you
must convey. Just now, as your ink-stained hand
dismays the financier who takes it, she
shudders, suffers visibly, shakes almost

imperceptibly her perfect head. You
always disappoint. The financier is
sterling—silver hair, silver tie, silver
tongue. He straightens a pearl-grey cuff, shares a
sober understanding with your friend. Three

questions he has for you: First, do you want
a cup of tea? (You do.) Next, do you want
this job? (You do. She's watching you.) And last,
in the third line of the third verse of the
third poem of your third book, what do you

mean by the rose? Oh God, and you only
remember the one, the book of traitors,
the book of worms. You always disappoint.
He sighs. He cuts from the trellis above
his desk a single bloom: camellia, Pink

Perfection, its halo of petals, its
crown of gold. He observes, "You are like this
Rose, intricate but doomed to failure." Your
friend shakes her head, grim fairy at the feast.
She knows what's best for you. Poor Briar Rose.

Oralee Dantzler

Watching the peonies
blowsy and flushed, she thought
I can do that. Could she?

Mirrors bloomed with her face,
with stolen peonies—
cool gray eyes, ivory cheeks.

Doves and sparrows. Closets
twitter and coo. Watching
the dove tree, its tissue

leaves, she trembled. Could she?
Shredded and bruised—not she—
leaves littered the grass, pale,

blown. Watching the roofers,
their angled jaws, she thought
I'll change my name, I'll be

Oralee Dantzler, I'll
go where I please. Roofers
lie down for her. They say

Oralee, Oralee.
My mother calls her loose,
I call her brave. Who knows

who she loves now, who knows
who she leaves—mimosa
breezy in cheap chintz, ripe,

always waving goodbye.

Gazelles

Two girls in silk kimonos, both
Beautiful, one a gazelle.
—W. B. Yeats

Whenever I see them they're nuzzling each other—
lips finding fingers, an arm flung round a neck,
their mouths gone slack with it,
their eyes bright on me.

They're not lovers. They live together.
One of them sleeps with men.
I think of the women I've lived with,
how careful we are—two single beds,

two typewriters. Did I drink your milk?
Anne and Diane circling each other,
pigeons on a lawn. Is that my scarf?
Did I eat your plums?

Bob. Coo. A woman with sky on her chest,
with an eye like opals. No one knew
what we wanted. Kimonos,
matching. Silk. Rice paper.

The lovers I've had, the lovers I've wanted—
not one innocent eye. Hide it,
my mother said. We always did,
a dark lantern. Anne and Diane, circling.

Twin beds in a dorm room, both
afraid in the dark. Whenever I see you
we circle each other, not sure
when to touch. Shivering, skittish,

our eyes for each other. Share, share alike.
Was he my lover? No one could touch.
Your scarf? My plums?
How careful we are.

They're not lovers. They nuzzle each other.
No circling: encircling. How careful
we are, our eyes for each other,
their eyes bright on me.

Lost Sisters

When she died her keys came to me in the mail,
Stiff refugees clacking with news.
One by one I laid them out—
Lost sisters, one for each door.

How Julie turned, still clutching the knob,
Chilled by what she had come to;
How Nanna's eyes tipped toward the light
However hushed the footfall;

And Lidy, plucking at frail chenille,
Shocking in toothed resemblance—
Oh Anne, Anne, we will be lost.
The jewelled threads, the fading dresses,

The letters stuck idly with pins—
What had she given me?
Tracts illuminated with dark horses,
Draggled crinolines wrapped in tissue,

The stained slip kept dark among the cardigans—
All hearts open, no secrets hid.
Oh who will wash away the stain?
Look out for me, Anne. Oh Anne, look out.

Talking Sickness

I don't know, it's hard to explain. I mean,
there's this woman who touches herself all day.
"Charlie," she says. She lies in a crib. "Charlie,
come on now. Come into me." The nurses
shift her to change the sheets. Miss Sugar
they call her. "That's enough now," they say.

You know what I mean? There's this woman
who sits in a chair. "Like my hair-do?" she says.
"Did it myself." She folds her kleenex
precisely in three. The nurses wink.
"Eat up, Mrs. Fitz. Come on now," they say.
She tucks the kleenex into her sleeve.

"Tuckered." She likes that word. "Working all day."
The nurses help her up, cut off the tv.
"I don't know," she says. Unbuttons her blouse.
"It'll be interesting to see." There's this nurse.
Worked at the VA—know what I mean? Men
held her hand. Grown men. "Sugar," they'd say.

"I don't know," she tells me. She touches her hair.
It's beige now. Her lipstick matches her nails.
"Hard to explain. Guess it's time to retire.
It'll be interesting to see." The nurses
wink. "Look here, Mrs. Fitz. Look who's come to see."
"Tuckered," she says. Hard to explain. Know what I mean?

Afterlife

When we found there was no room we came back to our
selves, though the fit already had slipped from the true.
Edging a foot into last year's shoe—the vamp cracked
by a summer's swollen instep, the heel turned with
a winter's drumming, the in-sole fusty—it was
like that, like thrift-store polyester, pilled and sagging.

While some shrugged back into what they'd out-worn,
no wonder some jostled for anything new,
grabbing the goods on the bargain counter,
leaving fresh souls empty-handed. Settling
smug into stolen dress, still they wore
the gun-shot's bloom over the right ear, the mark
of a palm on the left cheek, squinting spite,
wincing trust, the stab in the back.

One way or another, the self haunts the self,
outstaying its welcome. Contrary impulses
quarter a life, and absence beckons
with familiar hands. The voice—I'd know her anywhere—
never speaks again. The glance lost forever
in shuttling recurrence crosses the crowd
as if in ether. And a cat's weird cry—maroo, maroo—
though dead these many days, and the gulf between us.

Nymph

Swerving to miss a swell of forget-me-nots, the mower
shears the statue's toes. Now parted lips and half-shut eyes
show for what they are: not rapture, not even anguish,
but sheer dumb-struck shock; and her lichened flesh, dove-grey
with kindly weathering, turns ashen, lackluster
against the alabaster wound. And not the first time—

her lopped arms long since too numb to brush the sparrows
from her hair, or freshen the bloom of a chaplet
long since indiscriminate from curl; her lap of moss
long since too dull to coax a clacket from a broken
tambourine. And what could Procne finally do
but swallow, take it as it comes: life, trouble, change.

Slitting her eyes against the blaze of buttercups,
the migraine of suns cools to mere milky way: star-
gazing, how you look at it. Each ridged and needled leaf
of nettle pools with red, bleeds lady-bird stigmata
pulsing into air. And everywhere, laurel to narcissus,
dragonfly to damsel, hart's tongue to maiden's hair

breathes metamorphosis. Where by night the slit-eyed fox
Vulpecula bites through her bones to follow Grus
the crane, and Grus eyes Piscis Volans, the winged fish
gasping in air. Where out of the sea the silver
constellations rise, spangled with pain, crying
nymph, nymph: forget me not, remember me.

The Dream of the Horoscope

You have a friend who shares your birthdate, and
night by night she follows in the stars the life
you lead together. When the stars say "Fly!
she flies, and worries for you. When the stars
say, "You will meet a handsome stranger," she's

happy for you, curious what he's like,
musing late in her new love's arms. The stars
have taken her to Buenos Aires, where
she looks for you in vain. They've taken her,
more times than one, out of this world—and why

do you never greet her there, in the streets
of gold? Here is a postcard from Nepal:
"The stars say we will meet on the heights. What
stranger do you love now?" You climb the stairs
to your office, looking for a stranger

to love. When the stars say "Fly," you go home.
Who knows why paths diverge? You've danced on
waters she's never crossed—that shimmy when
the trough catches the light, and then the long
yearning. Who do you love? The boat set rocking

when you parted is rocking still, years gone,
the flex of your foot still springing through the
grain of its sprung ribs, the water lapping
still, running to shore in your long wake. The stars
say "Dance!" and she flies to Rio, while you

sleep in the quick-quick-slow of your murmuring
heart. Who do you love? The house is empty,
the stars silent. On the pillow beside
your head, Scheherazade, the books of dead men
open their blue lips, tell their strange lies.

Star

When she came from the movies she was someone else,
her lips re-set in a different line, a mouth you
might kiss, or might not dare to. Things got so crowded
that summer, she never knew when she opened the door
or the mirror, who she might see with her fresh eyes.

Lips twisting babyish into a coo,
gangsterish into a sneer, each stranger
finding her proper welcome. "James," she'd call, and
he'd come running, ever on tenterhooks
to face the guests, their haunting familiarity.

Yes, and the gangster's coo, the baby's sneer—
all the variations, one face sliding
into another in countless progeny.
"James," she'd call, guarding the star who's
reading the bones, riding the pulse of her blood.

Double Take

I.

It took me by surprise. The salesgirl said,
"If you don't put that up you'll lose that thing,"
nodding her head at the wallet left open
on the counter between us, and I obeyed:
I lifted it. You would have too—that motherly
concern, peremptory: If you don't wear a coat,
clean up that mess, put down that book . . . .
I was brought up right. I do what I'm told.

Nearly a hundred there. I paid
with some other woman's twenty, fumbling
the familiar rituals: where she'd
tuck the sales slip, where she'd keep her change—
a strain to think it through without appearing to,
to keep my hands where they belonged now, out of
my own cash, my own routines. When I snapped
the change compartment shut, a dime spun silver

through the air. I didn't wait to see what
face it turned, didn't breathe at all
in my headlong bolt, breakneck but circumspect,
out of linens to the parking lot, out
of the lot and home: my getaway. No,
she was breathing for me, urgent, dumb-struck—
back-seat driver wrenching her neck at stop-signs,
pumping at brake and gas, pedals to the floor.

Locking the doors like that, drawing the shades,
palms sweaty on the couch—it was like
kissing a stranger, cheating on your man.
I laid her bit by bit on the cushion
beside me: this covers you, this crosses you,
this crowns your enterprise. She must hate
the bland face on her license as much as I
hate mine—that's one good turn I did her. Behind the zip

where I keep family, she kept empty
promises: you will cross the great water,
you will overcome hardships, you will find
your desire in the due course of time.
Good luck, long life, happiness. I began
to shop from her lists, uncertain where to send
the strange gifts, how to prepare the foods. Even
after I destroyed the evidence—the charge cards

cut to ribbons, the checks ripped to bits
and flushed away—I traced her signature for
hour after hour: the tight curves, the bold strokes,
the strenuous backhand. Nothing to gain
by it, beyond the discipline, the muscles
racked back underhand against the grain, wound
around her little fingers. I probably even
smell like she does—the exertion, the anxiety,

paying the bills. In the due course of time
I'll drive down her block. I know she'll be there,
leaning on a rake, hand shading her eyes—I know
how her joints ache, how the light hurts her. I'll wave
and she'll wave back—nothing to lose—frowning
into the sun, puzzling it out: the turned face
of a hard stranger, the face she's never met,
that's now grown so familiar.

II.

The minute I walked in I saw the one I wanted—
trim, petite, made to fit a small palm. The guy
was sullen, never saw me sizing her. The skew
of his muscles, the squint of his brows—it was
quite a show, easy to read: the kind who screws
his own plans and then broods about it. The kind
who's pointedly not rude to every waitress.
The kind whose twisted back screams "Coddle me—

I dare you to, I dare you not to." Oh yes,
I said, I can read you like a book, read it,
read it and weep. A sullen guy, his face averted
so dogmatically, his neck ropes itself
like a noose. A most reliable accomplice.
I mean, with him refusing her eye,
what can I say? it was easy
for me to catch it. Easy, easy—

play the fish before you beach her. The thinnest ghost
of a sympathetic smile, the hair's breadth twitch
of an eloquent brow—the come-on
so subtle she can't be sure she's seen it,
the meeting of minds so fugitive
she won't recall the phantom of rapport.
Now the hook's set, I can let her do the rest:
lowered lashes, side-long glance—the looking

and not looking. Feeling her interest clench
its hand on my arm, I make my move
alive to the blocking cues, the sight-lines
between us: the dropped napkin, the lifted check,
the frank face held to the light, the generous
smile for the waitress, the casual drift her way,
close, closer, lips parted as if to speak—
everything to keep her eyes on my face

and not my hand. The merest jostle
and I'm out of there, my palm well-filled,
crossed—you might say—with silver. I laughed
to think of him growing still more sullen
in her disappointment, twisting himself
into a sneer in her loss, the spectral
flirtation fading as she realized
what lay between them was long gone.

I always take the snaps in as a kind of prize,
meeting the mugs I've cheated. I knew what I'd see—
a sullen guy in a dozen twisted poses,
interspersed, when she couldn't bear it, with
the mountains or the sea. But shot after shot
showed my own face, impeccable, playing
the con. Well, when you're seen, you're seen. I got
out of town. But I keep them still. A souvenir.

Three Small Epiphanies:

1. Swallowing Pearls

Some roll. Some shuttle like sesame.
Mussels gape. Spitlings someone might thread
seed your palm: milk seed. Swan teeth. Mustard.

Someone might thread the lavender strands,
might suck the milk, snuffle the swan's neck.
Magnolia pales, chokes. What's seeded you?

Wine dancing the frying pan, bright-eyed
pin-prick globes. I swallow whatever
you dish up. Pearls before swine. Lovely.

2. Spoiling

Sour coffee, milk turning in it. That
sort of day. Egg-tarnished. Butter-rancid.
Bile won't be sugared.

Though they tried, spoon after spoonful,
one cradling the sugar bowl, one crooning "You'll
spoil her."

Eleanor. She spoiled. Or someone did.
The neighborhood's rank with it—
The clinging vines, the blackening tomatoes.

Blame it on the weather, your
storm in a tea cup. There'll be showers,
there'll be shattered roses.

Oh la. Love's got a lot to answer.

3. Cold Sweat

Dangerous air, hot and cold at once,
chasing its tail through the azaleas.
Something sleek and vigorous, something
panting, shivery—fang in its mouth,
claw in its wing, sting in its tail: whip
in Persephone's dark bedroom. Like

meeting the one your old flame loves now—
no use in recalling how happy
you might have been. You're going to learn
to do without lushness, to do without
yawning roses. It's Colorado
vaporous at mid-day, Mojave

with the sun plunging: hot blood, cold heart,
air with a nip and a blister. You'll
learn from Shadrach, frost in the furnace.
No more gardenias. What we've got now
is chills and fever. The leaves turn up
their silver tongues. The wind says Ah.

Five Unexpected Harmonies:

1. Comet

Thrush chuffs, clears its throat: Comet. Comet.
Dark fields beyond Cambridge. Duet. Triolet.

New velvet shorn, old velvet sheen. Pheasants knotting the fields.
Back and forth: stitch, stitch. The quilt undulates.

Damp night in the parishes. The nightjar clicks its steel.
Between the frost and the field-glass, what glints your eye?

Perky. Perky. Comb out your tungsten hair.
In the hot dark above Mexico its tangles spark the air.

2. Tourist

They were wrong about travel, how it loosens the tongue.
Hands across the tea-table, the Bastille falling once more
beyond the Channel, she couldn't muster the merest
parlez-vous to buck the fusillade of syllable.
Cheek by jowl, Gallic mère et fille—or was it bru—
fired eloquent glance and shrug her way, exchanged
furious volleys of surmise. Nothing to reply.
No longer any words for her in any language she knew.

The gap-toothed, she'd heard, could fly when they willed.
No doubt it was so for some. The Canterbury Tea Shoppe
jam-packed with the well-travelled, ruddy with woolens:
any one of them could hand round the gâteaux, glad hand
a stranger into open-armed bonhomie. Oh yes,
their migrant teeth were good for a few miles more. While hers
clenched her face vapid, choked down the larynx's how-de-do.
She'd fly if she could, but where had flying got her?

"All the way to Charleston on that lip." What Daddy said
Brother says now, and his kids will say it too. She cracks
her brain for what she knows by heart, for what tips the tongue
that nags to be loosed: silence as souvenir, what Dad
didn't say. She's seen pouting since then, the genuine thing.
She knows how far an expert can go. Mother's peevish,
daughter's got the sulks: someone's soured the tea. What's
happened to her whatsit, her je ne sais quoi? Who's to say?

3. Mad Girl

I never knew how tuneful simple speech might be
until at the concert, right out loud, her speaking
shattered the Poulenc. Like a second cello,
a cello's ghost, playing its half-life out behind times.
Like looking for Echo, a shock to find her
speaking for herself now, her own Narcissus.

The ethereal turning out too fleshed for us,
recrimination was bound to follow. Miss Who
elbowed the thick waist; Mrs. Thing shook the thick wits
with a finger's metronome. We buttoned her up,
contention still ticking inside her, her rages
half-sung. I imagine her walking it out, beating

the pavement into time. The neighbor's boy
raises an eyebrow, raises a lip. The burden
begins again, insistent, inexorable—a tune
she can't shake from her head. We won't compose her,
though we got what we looked for—the harmonies,
the deliberated dissonance, the measured silence.

Pity, shutting her up—the Poulenc less witty
without her ostinato. It's her I remember,
her shoulders hunched, her little braid stiff with resentment:
no word for us, no note of it ever spoken
for us. It sticks to the mind, her recitative, wordless
but articulate, a tune no one else could carry.

4. Eclipse

Playing into the shadow, the pianist
inks his fingers, then his thumbs, then shakes them clear.
Slipping up his hands like mourning gloves, shadow
deepens the lined knuckles, dyes the fine bright hairs,
darkens the half-moons of his nails. It always

happens like this, false night duping the aircraft
back to their nests. At first glance one of the swifts,
another clipped black leaf shearing hairs from the thatch,
the spitfire kept its scimitar silhouette, the creed
of its open mouth. Moon in a net, sun

in a cup, yellow ball rushing the wicket—
any prodigy can predict what's rising
behind him. Oh honey, the hairs of your head
were always numbered, the heel stone long since set.
The keyboard's a palimpsest, black rising from white.

5. Lady Chapel at Ely

You'd expect a voice to thin in all that air
and thin it does, thins to fleshlessness, to a luster
glossing the vaulted spaces, a tone you might see through—
and yet it hangs there. The singer's parted lips
squeeze shut, her eyelids lower, her head inclines:
the carol's done. And still it hangs, her sheer last note—

bodiless yet curiously bodied. Sigh on sigh
the breathy organ—voce velata—spreads its veils
for one last song, Carissimi's lament for Mary
Stuart. The singer parts her lips, and note on note translucid
hangs against the veils of breath, one showing through the next,
fine drawn into thin air. Mary—not queen and yet queen,

thus like her namesake—came to her death
          in chic slashed sleeves,
the purple showing unrepentant through the black. Still,
Carissimi loves her, despite her two lost crowns, her
three lost kings, her stockings clocked with silver. Above us
four notes hang, the chord they make—"a morire"—solid
as any nimbus. So some say even after death

her lips moved, praising the Virgin. Why not? Old passions
die hard, and this room proves it: among its numbered saints,
affronted or addorsed, shepherdess or queen, not one
has kept her head; and every deep niche rippling the walls,
each nodding ogee—cusped, canopied, and crocketed—
stands empty, yearning, immaculate as any womb

or ear, as eager to be filled. You'd expect the dark
to rise in all this air, and rise it does, daggering
the mullions, knotting the reticulations,
complicating what persists in clunch of the Virgin's
life and miracles. And yet when the vast clerestory—
netted in milky glass and darkening with the rest—

gives sudden birth to unexpected birds, clarity
hangs there, bodiless yet curiously bodied; sky
vitrifies, an air you might see through; Carissimi
suspends our unbelief. In all this, no wonder mere
words go flat or faint, baffle the listener, shrivel, fall
on deaf ears, while note on note the vibrant song lives on.

IV

The Dream of Fresh Blood

You have a friend who always knocks too soon,
always has some place to go. He wants you
out of the house, out of the bath, before
you've got the towel well around you, before
the lather's out of your eyes, so eager to run

you're bleeding again. You can feel it, gouts
the size of walnuts, gouts the size of eggs
sliding from the cornucopia you are,
staggering harvest, matting the thick terrycloth,
blackening your thighs, freckling the leather seats

of his convertible. It's all his fault
you're ahead of yourself, and you want him
to slow down, park at the curb, sit tight, meet your
expectations. But he's no husband, he's
your friend, so eager to make it up he

gives you the shirt off his back. It suits you,
that worn flannel, that black tartan with its
one red thread, a geometric blood line
pulsing you dry as you're cooling your heels,
biding your time, waiting for him to bring

what he thinks you need, you in your skirt of
scarlet. But he's no husband, he's your friend,
never comes when he's called. You're so eager
by the time he's there, blood streams from his hands
and feet, he's bleeding again, you can't take

your eyes from the blood. And maybe you're meant
to be together, maybe you even want
each other. Admit it. So there's a black dog
guarding your doorstep. He's there to be fed.
This is one intruder he'll always let in.

Loose Woman

Just how promiscuous were you? he asked,
catching sight of my *Bluffer's Guide to*
Masturbation. A fair question, if
unanswerable—anything one might say
already weighted: thumb on the scale,
extra finger in the pie. Well, fair game—

like others of my kind, I used to
keep lists—the broncs I'd bucked, the fish I'd scaled,
the ones who'd kiss and tell. There was this guy—
met him in church, and shocked to discover
an atheist like himself—used to compute
weekly box scores, tallies, inventories

of all his favorite tunes since 1961,
and a mind like that will quantify
whatever it embraces. I confess
with some chagrin that I stopped counting
when the permutations proved me flagrantly
innumerate. So Freud found women dull

for all their perversity, their by-play
on the couch: all they dream about is love,
he whined. Nothing to puzzle out. My dreams
speak for themselves: all I dream about
is nuts: walnuts, almonds, cashews, filberts,
macadamias, brazils, pistachios—

all the pecans denied me since the
allergy set in. Don't smirk. I know it's
metaphoric. Still, for all he's got me
dead to rights, for all the id flaps
its semaphores, stool pigeon waggling
the body's tongue, I like how it changes,

deviance in the dumb show. It's like
switching to a bikini in mid-season,
the jigsaw you become provocative
to some, distracting to others. Fixated
on the piece he recognized, he told me
Love, I've got the picture. And did anyone

ever mention your blue eyes? I'll tell you
what I thought: not again. Where every married man
sees the wild blue yonder, the azure, the way
out of there, and every bachelor
the bone-rimmed blue pools at LaBrea,
the there to be out of. Still, there are lines

and lines. My favorite is the one at the
filling station, where I stood in a pool
of petrol back in 1974,
and he said—the nozzle slobbering
over the flank of the fender—Honey,
been pumping your own gas long?

Choker

Have 'em out, Pops says. But he's too late—
they don't do that anymore. What you've got
you keep: the thorn in the side, the lash
in the eye, the swelling finger
down the throat. You live with it. I've learned to.

A gem cut so its facets edge the air,
bladed scintillations. What's a necklace for—
bringing tears to the eye, a girl to her knees?
Bedded so deep in her neck, the slightest quiver
turns her husky: gem of the first water.

Ice needs shaking before it ramifies.
The finger lakes lay wet for hours, cold
but open, til here a leaf falls, there a fin
breaks water: and the goose-flesh pellicle
needles a whip-stitch clash of long-eyed sharps—

and just as fast dissolving. Have a good
cry, she told me, pleased to see my throat knit up,
my spindrift eyes. Good cry, bad cry: there's
no loosing it, this choker still jerking me around.
Lump in the throat. You live with it. I've learned to.

Bad Love:

1. Beat

If he does beat her, I hope he will do it tenderly.
It may be that a little of it will suit her fevered temperament.
—*Anthony Trollope,* The Last Chronicle of Barset

The green rain beat its sharp tattoo.
She had to strain to hear him. Like
to, he said. Like you to. She shook
her head no. Not many do, he

said. She thought of her man, his blue
tattoo. You're the one, he says. You
fly off the handle. Smash tables.
Punch walls. Hot head. She shook. No. No.

Wanted to show him. Pitch into
him. Belt. Slug. The spunk flared, fuse lit.
Racket. Rap. Rage. Thought of her dreams,
jaw jutted, teeth clenched against him.

The poke. The pinch. The smack. The jab.
Thought of the calculated slap.
Now. Again now. His smug mouth, his
dead eyes. Look at me. Look at me.

2. Gossip

Words, words have digged our grave.
—Laurence Binyon, "Tristram's End"

Pillow talk, you might have called it,
though they kept the sword between them in the bed.
A hard line drawn straight, uncompromising,
through the center of the heart-to-heart.

But how the bed-sheets rustled! what they
kept under wraps! when she let her hair down,
when he unbuttoned. Let's not mince words: she
was open-mouthed. He pricked his ears.

The closer she leaned the more he strained
to listen. Her whisper skimmed his cheek; his
murmur grazed her chin. How he relished her
chit-chat, her tittle-tattle. How she burned

for the buzz in her ear. Squeezed to a
hair's breadth, cleaving still to the line: sweet talk,
hear say. Blood on his lips, on her white hands.
Blood on the sheets—no wonder you mistook it.

3. Thrall

How patient his hand through the dead hours of winter—
finger to thumb: pinched crust, tattered cheese,
smidgens and scrimptions coaxed inchmeal over the sill
for red-breast or speckled throat drawn snick by snip
at last to the rich crumb in the long palm.

So it felt like his gift, like grace rebounding
to the giver's hand, as gradually
the chill sheets warmed, and our bleached breath
cleared in the warming air, and as dusk came on
the volatile robin, the breath-taking thrush
gave what they had to give.

It seemed the very bed would break with it
as I was breaking, a dry husk splitting
into song. And no one has to tell me
what anyone might see: what felt like grace
or amity, gratitude or grief
had more to do with need, with greed, with territory.

4. Trust

"Why don't you trust me?" he asked, her first hint
that she shouldn't—beyond his post cards from
the zoo, that night with the leather boys, his
nasty endearments. Looking for trouble,
she'd found him, what she wanted at the time,
evidently, she supposed. Trust him? He'd

ridden the waves south, married a wrestler,
rustled tornadoes, fucked the IRA;
now he yearned for a war zone, for Moslem
adventure, for shit in the streets, to be
the best hostage. She set out the icons—
James Dean, Elvis, John Lennon, JFK—

if you couldn't trust them, who could you love?
She couldn't see where she'd gone wrong: so fine
a line between crusader and dick-head,
rebel and misfit, the tortured and the
torturer. She thought of that first glimpse,
how interesting he seemed—the fall of hair

that might have masked a scar, the favored leg
that might have masked a wound, how brave and true
he made her feel—though from the very start she
masked, hid, favored, fell. If your eye offend—
but where would she be without a blind eye?
without dark desire leading her, trusting, on?

5. Desire

We drove out to the city of the dead
where he showed me how the fire blazed through.
You can trace its path over the flagstones,
up the black brick steps still braced by iron
rails and pickets, out onto the cold slab

of the foundations. The heavy trees stand
charred clean, burnished. A palm crests the hill,
its fronds crisped to stubs, its fat bulk bronzed
to a pineapple finial, announcing
hospitality. No rule to it—

how it eats one house and spares another,
skipping this tiled roof and that stained window.
A small-boned cat might kindle in a breath,
but here he comes, mewing for his supper,
and here is a widow, come to feed him.

So he said to me, now you've seen it.
Would you still wake the dragon? Around us
the scorched earth cracked its hoard, every rise bright
with basket-of-gold, hyacinth, lapis, pearl.
Ash lit my tongue. God forgive me, I said yes.

Following Fred Astaire:

"I was never a good ballroom dancer. I've even had complaints about it."

—Fred Astaire, quoted in Tim Satchell's Astaire: The Biography

for Marjorie Murphy

1. No Kisses

> *"Widowers like myself are in a touchy position. If I go out with a young woman and she's very attractive, very lively, very capable of making me forget sadness, then people say I'm robbing the cradle. If I go out with some woman of my own age, they say I'm concentrating on grandmothers. Very difficult."*

From the depot to the edge of town he's
on about his prostate. From there to the hotel
it's his desire. Nothing to do with me
for all your rolling eyes, Miss Sue: it's just
spilled out, an open tap, a brimming tub.
I know how he feels, how all this time he's been
dancing with strangers, never putting a foot wrong,
and now it's gone: partner me, partner me.

Nothing to do with you or me, Miss Sue,
the voice in the next apartment. Night after night
the reasonable complaint—"Lonely, so lonely"—but
by day she's uppity, snubbing the gay
divorcees. Mrs. Jones, on for eighty,
still has her figure, still cuts the rug—Antoine's
best partner. Truly: never a foot wrong,
even when he's mocking, "dancing with Granny."

Granny draws on her silk stockings, tightens
her garters, turns to the glass, her eyebrows
ironic on cradles she might rob. She likes
to dance, would like to meet some dancing widower
though—don't get me wrong—Antoine is fine for
what he is. She puts her hand on his shoulder
and follows, in spite of all she knows and he can't
foresee. Forget sorrow? Miss Sue, she's seen that movie.

2. Dancing With Your Sister

Adele, picking up the mannerisms of the dancers she observed, was fast developing into a juvenile lead and increasingly looked an unsuitable partner for her kid brother. Inevitably, one day a theatre manager reported, in a phrase that was to haunt Fred for many years afterwards: "The girl seems to have talent but the boy can do nothing."

So Little Kit and Baby Rachel made
the reception, charmed the priest and startled
the band. "That's no hokey-pokey" the sax cried,
while the drummer's "Put your little foot"
tapped itself right out. No, no nursery rounds:
even infants rise to the passionate
occasion, spurred by song, by dancing eyes.
Bride and groom upstaged in their own cake-walk,

on their own cake-stand. So the bride takes Kit
on her hip, leans into a fox-trot, undulates
a rumba, cha-chas a bit, and dips and dips him.
So the groom spins Rachel out of her self,
goes down on his knees, turns under her arm.
Kit dances with an uncle, Rachel with an aunt—
anything goes in this wild fandango.
Anything goes. The boy can do everything.

Signifying matrimony, no? The bride
dances better with her brother, and the groom
doesn't resent it yet, that fluency.
Kit and Rachel snap their baby fingers,
bend their dimpled knees, bask in celebrity.
So there's a tug of war in their clasped hands.
What else is new? You can't have the cat's whiskers
or miaow without sharp claws, sharp teeth, sharp eyes.

3. Cheek to Cheek

His attitude is understandable—having had the perfect partnership with Adele he didn't want a partnership with anyone else—he was caught in the dilemma of needing a partner, yet wanting to do it alone. In some ways he achieved that by rehearsing with his male collaborator, Hermes Pan, taking Ginger Rogers' role.

Anyone can wear the fresh face, bat the lashes,
make the goo-goo eyes, playing at first love, calf love,
true love. What's tricky is to get the deep sunk tug,
the wrench infinitesimal, that makes it right,
that makes it clear it's meant, and meant to last, to be.
Then you can walk on air, dance on ceilings, swing your
many partners: then it's love, again. Any school girl
knows that in the right arms the kitchen maid turns queen,

so if the shoe's bloody, you keep it to yourself.
Swept off my feet, again, head over heels, I can
rest a minute from the labor of it: mauled corns,
cramped arches, blistered toes. He's under my skin, again,
so I itch with it, hanker to shake it out, kick
it off, shimmy it away—in tune, again, with
a plunked and twanging heartstring. Flashy steps, fast turns:
always someone—thank God—between me and my desire.

The turned head, the flushed cheek, the blinded eye; the skin
aware and wary beneath the traitor silk; the waist
gripped tight til breath heaves the breasts free; the arched back
dragging the head behind, sweeping the floor with hair;
the weak flesh trembling, breath wrung, red rose bled white, thigh
opening involuntary; each step launching
the next, inexorable: yen, rut, bruising, dismay.
I could dance it by myself, what love's done to me.

4. Top Hat

"I make love with my feet," Astaire said, when asked why the couple did not kiss on screen in the first seven of their films.

When the dead leave, no one defends them. "Your mother,"
says Nannie, "couldn't wring out a wash rag," and it
may be true, for all I remember. It didn't
matter at the time—you can tell from his eyes here,
for once without their glasses, and happy to be
short-sighted. Their skin incandescent with dancing,
they've turned their flash on the camera, searing the film,
burning their way through the buff envelope, the socks

and shorts, the very bureau drawer that held them, back
into light—impractical, defenseless. Last time
I danced with Bob, he was three and riding my hip
to the Beatles' "Til There Was You." For all that time
lost—and it's no wonder, raised in the same South—we
do a mean shag, jitterbug manqué, just risqué
enough to know we've done it right. Or wrong. Black sheep
cavorting, indefensible. Not an easy

man to talk to, our daddy, but you should see him
dancing. The father of the groom tonight, he lights
the floor with his soft shoe, parts the air with his tails,
spins his wife—Bob's mother—til she's beaming, his feet
clearly on the ground, his past so far behind him
it can't reach to tap his shoulder. Couples dancing:
he folds it to his heart, this life, and turns it
like a cane. Leading man or no, needs no defending.

The Dream of Eros

You have a friend who travels incognito,
who comes and goes under cover of dark,
who wears a mask to bed. Out of the shadows,
lilies on the wind, rose petals drifting
into your hands, your sleeping arms: "Expect me

when you see me." (You may as well enjoy
a joke so sweetly double-edged.) In between,
you're left with busy-work—the grains of rice,
the automatic writing, the black river
to swim again and again. You're ready

for the test, for the pool to swallow you,
ready for the night to twist in your hand,
ready to be seared awake, but beauty
keeps itself dark. A ring of braided hair,
breath stirring through your lips: "You'll know me

when you see me." (Another joke, when
every face seems likely, but turns out wrong.)
You've got sentries at the borders, you've got
spies in the alley-ways, but love slips in
and out before your eyes can open.

Always some spoiler handy with a box
for empty dreams, with mirrors to reflect on—
so many faces, so infinitely
superimposed. The trace of a caress
inscribed on your inner thigh: "You'll see me

when you least expect me." Oh sisters, sisters,
congratulate me, be happy for me.
In my alchemical marriage, the dark
beats heavy wings, the arrows are flying,
I lift my face, and love, love strikes its light again.

Notes

Walk Like a Man: "No can, no legs . . .": Holden Caulfield in J.D. Salinger's *Catcher in the Rye.*

Stick Shift: The "Sisters" in this poem are not nuns, but the "spiritual advisors" whose hand-shaped signs announce their ability to read palms throughout the rural American south.

Oralee Dantzler is a real person, a friend of my parents; but the poem bearing her name is not about her, at all. I wrote the poem because I love the name, and the remembered sound of Mrs. Dantzler's unusual voice.

Spoiling: "Eleanor . . .": see Ezra Pound, Canto VII.

Cold Sweat: "Persephone's dark bedroom": Sappho, from Fragment 20, "We put the urn aboard ship," in Mary Barnard's translation.

Following Fred Astaire: The quotations come from Tim Satchell's 1987 biography of Astaire.

Following Fred Astaire is the winner of the 1998 Word Works Washington Prize. Nathalie Anderson's manuscript was selected from 387 manuscripts submitted by American poets.

Final judges in this year's contest were Jim Beall, James Hopkins, *Assistant Director,* Martha Sanchez-Lowery, *Director,* Robert Sargent, and Hilary Tham.

First readers were Nancy Allinson, Donald Cunningham, Wayne Drozynski, Pat Gray, Tod Ibrahim, Sydney March, Steven B. Rogers, Maggie Rosen, Adela Sattori, Jonathan Vaile, Marie Wehrli, Rhonda Williford, and Marcella Wolfe.

Second readers were Karren L. Alenier, Jamie Brown, and Miles David Moore.

About the author

Born in Columbia, South Carolina, Nathalie Anderson was educated at Agnes Scott College, Georgia State University and Emory University. As a professor at Swarthmore College in the Department of English Literature, she teaches courses in modern and contemporary poetry and writing workshops in poetry. A chapbook of her poems, *My Hand My Only Map,* was published in 1978 by House of Keys Press. Her poems have appeared in such journals as: *Nimrod, Paris Review, Prairie Schooner,* and *Southern Poetry Review.* In 1986, she was a fellow at Yaddo; in1993, she was awarded a Pew Fellowship in the Arts.

Nathalie Anderson wrote the libretto for the opera *The Black Swan,* a collaboration with the composer Thomas Whitman, based on Thomas Mann's novella *Die Betrogene.* The opera was performed at Swarthmore College under Sarah Caldwell's direction in the fall of 1998. She has also collaborated with Orchestra 2001 on productions of Mozart operas for children and was one of four Philadelphia poets commissioned by the Concerto Soloists of Philadelphia to work with local composers and photographers in a multi-media performance of contemporary music patterned on Vivaldi's Four Seasons.

About the artist

Perky Edgerton received her Bachelor of Fine Arts from Boston University in 1978, and a Master of Fine Arts from Tyler School of Art in 1980. She has exhibited her work in numerous one-person and group exhibitions in Philadelphia, New York, and Chicago. She has been the recipient of several grants and fellowships, notably a National Endowment for the Arts Fellowship in 1982, and two subsequent Pennsylvania Council for the Arts Fellowships. Currently she lives in Swarthmore, Pennsylvania, with her husband and two daughters. She divides her time between family, painting, and teaching art at The School at Rose Valley.

About the Word Works:

The Word Works, a nonprofit literary organization, publishes contemporary poetry in collector's editions. Since 1981, the organization has sponsored the Washington Prize, an award of $1,000 to a living American poet. Each summer, Word Works presents free poetry programs at the Joaquin Miller Cabin in Washington, DC's Rock Creek Park. Annually, two high school students debut at the Miller Cabin Series as winners of the Young Poets Competition.

Since Word Works was founded in 1974, programs have included: "In the Shadow of the Capitol," a symposium and archival project on the African-American intellectual community in segregated Washington, D.C.; the Gunston Arts Center Poetry Series (including Ai, Carolyn Forché, Stanley Kunitz, Linda Pastan, among others); the Poet-Editor panel discussions at the Bethesda Writer's Center (including John Hollander, Maurice English, Anthony Hecht, Josephine Jacobsen, among others); Poet's Jam, a multi-arts program series featuring poetry in performance; a poetry workshop at the Center for Creative Non-Violence (CCNV) shelter, and the Writers' Retreat workshops and readings in Tuscany. In 1997 the Word Works began distributing chapbooks by Mica Press (Ft. Collins, Colorado) under a cooperative agreement.

Past grants have been awarded by the National Endowment for the Arts, the National Endowment for the Humanities, the DC Commission the Arts and Humanities, the Witter Bynner Foundation, and others, including many generous private patrons.

Word Works has an archive of artistic and administrative materials in the Washington Writing Archive housed in the George Washington University Gelman Library.

Please enclose a self-addressed stamped envelope with all inquiries. Find out more about the Word Works at

http://www.writer.org/wordwork/wordwrk1.htm